NATIVE PEOPLE ▲ NATIVE WAYS ▲ SERIES

VOLUME II
⟵ ⟶

▲▲▲

The
Native American
Book of

Life

▼▼▼

NATIVE PEOPLE ▲ NATIVE WAYS ▲ SERIES

VOLUME II

▲▲▲

The Native American Book of

Life

▼▼▼

TEXT BY

White Deer of Autumn

ILLUSTRATIONS BY

Shonto W. Begay

BEYOND
WORDS
Publishing
I   N   C

Beyond Words Publishing, Inc.
4443 NE Airport Road
Hillsboro, Oregon 97124-6074
503-693-8700
1-800-284-9673

Page Layout: The TypeSmith
Cover Design: Soga Design

Printed in Canada
Distributed to the book trade by Publishers Group West

The corporate mission of Beyond Words Publishing, Inc.:
Inspire to Integrity

Library of Congress Cataloging-in-Publication Data
White Deer of Autumn.
    The native American book of life / author, White Deer
of Autumn ; illustrator, Shonto W. Begay.
        p.   cm. — (Native people, native ways series ; v. 2)
    Summary: Focuses on the Native Americans' life with the
European settlers after Columbus and their attempt to retain
their culture and traditions in a changing, modern world.
    ISBN 0-941831-43-4 (v. 2) : $5.95
    1. Indians of North America—Children—Juvenile literature.
2. Indians of North America—Social life and customs—Juvenile
literature.   3. Indians of North America—Food—Juvenile literature.
[1. Indians of North America—Social life and customs.] I. Begay,
Shonto, ill.   II. Title.   III. Series: White Deer of Autumn. Native
people, native ways series ; v. 2.
E77.4.W48   1992 vol. 2
[E98.C5]
970.004'97 s—dc20
[970.01'1]   92-12269
                                                                      CIP

*These stories are dedicated
to Ray Fadden (Tehenetorens) and
to the memory of Princess Red Wing*

CONTENTS

◀——▶

PART I

The Children, Always the Children
▼▼▼

CHAPTER 1

←—————————→

Imagine a Nation . . .

Imagine a nation of people where children were never hit, never yelled at, and never even punished. Imagine a nation where children were treated with the same respect given to any adult, where the parents did nothing without thinking what was best for the children.

Imagine a nation where the adults made decisions keeping in mind not only the present but the unborn children of future generations as well. Imagine a nation where children were such a source of joy and love that the nation seemed to exist for the welfare of the children, always the children.

Such a nation did exist. Such nations did exist. They existed often without schools, and always without orphanages, juvenile deliquency centers, or day care. They existed without prisons or police. These nations were the American Indian nations of North and South America.

For a child of an Indian nation, education was ongoing, a lifetime of experience that began in the mother's womb. When a young Indian mother-to-be discovered she was pregnant, she began telling stories to her unborn child. She told about good times and hard times. She told of the supernatural Trickster and of the spirit beings who traveled from the stars. The stories explained past worlds and emerging new ones. The stories retold the Creation and the beginning of the People. They remembered relatives and heroes, dead and alive, and blood ties with other tribes. With these stories a child's education began before he or she was born.

Music was the rhythm of the stories, and the music helped the embryo to grow. Quite often parents sang to their unborn child. A future father might use a rattle or drum to accompany the stories being sung. Sometimes, out in the Great Plains late at night, a flute player would send a haunting melody through the village. As it floated through the air, it brought to each teepee a sense of peace and well-being. And the new mother, busy at her work the next day, would always take time to sing a melody to the child within her.

Even as they worked in the fields, the Wampanoag women of the Northeast coast and the Shawnee mothers of the Ohio Valley sang to their babies, both those stirring within their wombs and the little ones laced in colorfully beaded cradleboards. The cradleboards, suspended in the boughs of ancient trees, swayed in the gentle breeze.

"Rock-a-bye baby, in the tree top, when the wind blows, the cradle will rock . . . ," they sang.

Long ago the Pilgrims heard the native Wampanoag mothers singing this lovely lullaby to their babies. The Pilgrims translated it into English and began singing it to their children, using the Indian's soft melody. But only Indian babies ever rocked in their cradles from the boughs of trees.

From birth, song filled each Indian's life. Song helped to teach children. By learning the songs of the People and creating new ones, the children were assured of a way to express their deepest feelings.

Besides song, an Indian child was assured of one other thing: he or she would never be without a home and loving relatives. Often a mother's sister was regarded as a second mother. She was called "mother" too. Uncles, aunts, and grandparents also played important roles in raising children. Most everyone in the village had some influence in the child's rearing. If a child's parents tragically died, the child would live with the second mother or with other loving relatives.

To teach by example was the key in Native American tribal life. Adults acted the way they wanted children to act. Because little eyes are constantly observing and little ears are keen and attentive, Indian adults were careful to set good examples. Sometimes, even a good example can have adverse influence. Children *do* get into mischief.

When an Indian child misbehaved, the relatives didn't scold. They didn't spank. They certainly didn't beat the child. Parents, grandparents, and relatives alike would come up with other ways to help a child understand the dos and don'ts of tribal life.

Lame Deer, an old Lakota medicine man, in his book, *Lame Deer, Seeker of Visions,* described a time when he was a little boy. He watched an honoring ceremony for a little girl. The major part of the ceremony was having her ears pierced by a highly respected man of the tribe. Her parents honored this man by presenting him wonderful gifts of beautiful beadwork, blankets, and even a horse.

Lame Deer wanted to be honored in the same way. So, when he returned to the lodge of his parents, he found himself alone with his baby sister. He decided to pierce his own baby sister's ears. He held her down while he stuck an awl through her tiny lobes. She cried and screamed, kicked and twisted. Still, he was careful to do a good job, just the way he saw it in the ceremony.

Naturally, when his parents returned, they gasped in horror. Many of today's fathers would explode on the spot and the mothers would demand that the kid be punished. Such was not the case among the Lakota.

Instead, his father explained that what was done could not be undone. Her ears were pierced. Lame Deer had denied his parents and his sister the honoring ceremony that would have meant so much to them. So, to honor his sister in the tradition of the ceremony, Lame Deer had to have a "give-away." But a horse was the only thing he owned, given to him by his father the previous year. Lame Deer loved that horse more than anything else.

It hurt when he gave that horse away. Did it hurt! But Lame Deer learned about responsibility and about what real "give-aways" are all about.

Indian children were taught certain types of behavior, depending on the tribe. One behavior was taught by all tribes — respect for the elders. If children didn't show this utmost regard, they were quickly taken aside by their parents or relatives. The children weren't scolded. They were simply told what was proper and what was not.

In some cases, a child needed more than just being told to act right. They were reminded of the different powers in the world. Some of these powers sought out children who acted badly. In a Pueblo ceremony, one Katchina goes to the home of a misbehaving child. The Katchina demands to eat the child. The child's mother, of course, meets the Katchina at the door and pleads for her child's life. She asks for another chance and offers the Katchina raw meat instead. Relieved when the Katchina takes the meat, the trembling child is now anxious to act better.

Most Indian tribes had a version of the "boogeyman." Loud and disrespectful children were told by their parents that a horrible creature dwelled deep in the forests or the sea. He might come for them if they continued to misbehave. Among the Iroquois, stories of greedy flying heads with wide mouths and sharp pointy teeth were enough to make most children listen to their elders' advice.

Naturally, these stories of scary beings frightened the little ones into behaving. Older children sometimes thought they knew better. When they doubted the existence of such creatures, their parents told them that the white man or the missionaries would come and take them away. The older children knew this happened, and they listened.

It must have hurt the People beyond words and fueled the fires of war when they saw what the white man did to Indian children. How can words describe the feelings of Indian parents and elders who survived the burning of the Pequot Nation by the early English colonists? Can we imagine how they felt hearing the screams from their burning little ones? Can words describe how the Cheyenne and Arapaho dealt with the news of the soldiers burning their village and slaughtering their women and children at Sand Creek, a place where the Indians had been promised they could live in peace? Can words describe the agony of Geronimo when he returned to his camp and found his family all murdered, his little boy impaled on a soldier's sabre? Can words help us to understand what it must have been like when a Cherokee father had to carry the corpse of his son or his daughter and lie by it through the night because the soldiers would only let the Cherokee bury their dead every third day on the Trail of Tears? Can words help us to imagine the anguish of the People of the Lakota Nation when they searched the snowblanketed earth at Wounded Knee for the bodies of the Indian children massacred by the Seventh Cavalry soldiers? There are no words to describe the feelings of the People at those times.

It may be hard to imagine that these events happened to Native American nations where children were the

most sacred treasure. But they did happen. To watch the killing of their children, the future of the People, must have destroyed the hearts of the Indian parents and others of the tribe. To them, everything was for the children, always the children.

Raising their young to be honorable, loving, and responsible human beings was a sacred trust.

CHAPTER 2

Into Our Midst Has Come a New Life

▲▲▲

Ho! Ye Sun, Moon, Stars, all ye that move in the heavens, I bid you hear me!

Into your midst has come a new life. Consent ye, I implore!

Makes its path smooth, that it may reach the brow of the first hill!

> —from the Omaha Indian song,
>   "Introduction of the Child to
>   the Universe"

For Native Americans, birth was the most special occasion. Birth was the promise of the future. It meant the survival of the tribe. As each boy and girl grew and learned the tribal culture, they would help the People to continue.

Each tribe and nation had its own ways of acknowledging such a sacred event as a newborn's arrival among the People.

Charles Eastman, whose Dakota Indian name was Ohiyesa, wrote in *Indian Boyhood* about the birth of an Indian. When a boy was born among the Dakota (eastern Sioux), it was the custom for the brother to submerge himself in water, either from a cold lake or an icy stream. If the birth occurred in the winter, the brother then had to bathe naked in the snow. He would roll and tumble until he was completely wet. If the brother was too little for such acts, water was poured over him. If the infant had a sister, she was put into the water. This was to display their courage to the spirit of their new sibling.

Among some of the Indian nations, it was often the practice for the father to immerse the newborn itself into the water. If it were winter, the father would chip a hole in the ice and dip the baby into the chilly water.

These traditions helped make children stronger. They became better able to handle hardship very early in life. Also, a bath in water, the lifeblood of Mother Earth, impressed upon the young mind the importance of water. The baby began to learn that water is essential to life itself.

The Hopi Indians, like the Lakota, the Iroquois, and all Native American nations, believed that the arrival of a new life was an especially sacred event. According to Frank Waters's *Book of the Hopi,* a Hopi child was kept in darkness for twenty days after its birth in order to allow the spirit a chance to adjust to its new home.

On the first day of the infant's life, a husk of Mother Corn was placed beside him and remained there all the while. He was washed that first day with simmering cedar water. The sweetness of the water's scent filled the senses of the infant. After this sacred bath, the newborn was rubbed in the finest powder of white cornmeal. This was repeated throughout the twenty days. Much care was taken during this time to prepare the child for his introduction to the great Sun Father and Earth Mother.

On the day of the introduction, all the aunts arrived to support the baby's mother. First she passed husks of Mother Corn over the infant four times. With each pass she made a prayer for the child's well-being. On the first pass she gave the baby a name. This name was not necessarily the one the child would keep, as all the aunts had names too. The name most often used on that special day would ultimately be the one belonging to the child.

The Hopi infant was introduced to the Sun Father for the first time as the mighty sun rose above the eastern horizon and lifted the blanket of mist from Mother Earth.

In this way the Hopi child, like many Native American children, began to learn that though we have human parents, our real parents, the cosmic parents of the People, are the Sun and Mother Earth.

This introduction to the universe helped the parents to realize that though they were the human parents, they were also the guardians of a child of the Sun and Earth.

This meant that their responsibility for good parenting was a sacred trust.

As Indian children grew, they became aware that not only were they citizens of their individual tribes and nations, but they were also members of the universe. They were connected to all things, and therefore, they had a part in maintaining the balance.

Among many Native Americans it was important to bury the newborn's placenta. Since the placenta had sustained the unborn child in the mother's womb, it was returned to Mother Earth who sustains all her children. This returning was done with words of humble gratitude. Some women had their husbands place it into a river, knowing it would eventually return to one of the oceans and the saltwater womb of Mother Earth.

The umbilical cord, which is the part that eventually falls from an infant's navel, was usually put in either a plain deerskin pouch or one designed as a lovely beaded turtle. The turtle was a symbol of the child's lifeline. Although not all Native mothers in all tribes practiced this, they each did take special care of these things.

The turtle design was popular among people like the Ojibwa because the turtle lives long if it survives the first year. When sea turtles hatch from their eggs on the sandy shore, they immediately head for open waters. Most never make it, because they are devoured by sea gulls and crows. Of the few that do enter the sea, many become food for the larger fish. Any baby turtle that survives the first year, though, may live a hundred years or more.

There are other reasons the turtle was so important among the People. A turtle's heart is incredibly strong. The need for a strong heart was important among the People. There was also a spiritual link between the turtle and this land we live upon. Many Native American tribes and nations, such as the Mohawk, Seneca, Cherokee, and Paiute, believe that this continent was first formed on the back of a turtle. The turtle symbol was very important and powerful among the People. They used it as a form of protection and early influence for their children.

Some tribes used other types of pouches to store the umbilical cord. The Lakota sometimes made a pouch in the form of a lizard. This pouch was highly decorated and attractive. Its purpose was to fool or trick evil spirits that could harm or kill. Because an evil spirit would be drawn to the prettiest pouch, the umbilical cord was usually not placed in this one, but in another.

Once the infant has lived a year, the umbilical-cord bundle is no longer needed for protection. Some Indian mothers hold it as a keepsake. Other Indian mothers bury it in a secret place. Some of the old people today have said that if the umbilical cord were not kept or cared for in some way, an Indian could appear foolish, always searching for something.

For extra protection for their children, many Native parents hung dream catchers or dream wheels from their baby's cradle. They believed that these wheels prevented nightmares and that the web of the wheel caught evil before it disturbed and threatened the sleeping infant.

We are all familiar with the soft spot on the top of a newborn's head. It pulsates, almost like breathing. Many Native Americans believed that this pulse was a soft-sounding rhythm that allowed the infant to maintain direct communication with the Great Mystery. Some believed that the spirit which entered the new body, and which was still part of the Mystery, entered through this opening. At death, it left through this same door. Of course, for the child's protection, the soft spot hardened quickly. Later, the Indian child would discover his voice and would learn that he could reestablish that same communication with the Great Mystery through prayer and singing.

Quite often the baby's spirit was not completely anchored to its body. The spirit could drift away from the body. For this reason, a little medicine pouch or even the dream wheel would serve to keep the spirit close to the body.

All these precautions the People felt were necessary to ensure the survival of their infants. The Indian knew that there were mysterious powers in the world. All things are a part of the Great Mystery, but not all of them are for the good of the People.

Today, modern medicine is still puzzled by something called "crib death." For unknown reasons, a perfectly healthy newborn will die in its sleep. This was the kind of thing that Native American parents sought to protect their children from. For them, the magic of the pouch and dream wheel worked well enough that it is used even today!

Another vital part of an infant's life was its cradle-board. Some people in modern times call it a *papoose*, which is a real Indian word.

The cradleboard was usually decorated with beads or colorful porcupine-quill flowers and butterflies — both symbols of new life and beauty. A circular piece of wood protected the baby's head. From it dangled feathers, bright beads, and even a dream wheel. These were fastened for spirit power. They also helped develop the infant's eyes, kept his attention, and made him familiar with the things of this world. Today, modern versions of these dangling objects are called mobiles.

The cradleboard kept the baby secure. He couldn't thrash about or wander away from his mother. It allowed him to feel comfortable, wrapped in loving protection and beauty.

Sometimes the infant was propped up against the wall of a lodge. Sometimes the newborns were suspended in their cradles from shady tree boughs, as the Wampanoag women did when they tended their gardens. Gently they would rock in soft breezes. From their cradleboards, the babies could see what was going on in their new world. They knew that their relatives were always close at hand.

The cradleboard helped the young mother. With it she could carry the baby on her back. This was convenient, because it allowed her hands to be free for other uses. It's also much easier to carry a baby in this fashion. In the 1960s and '70s, many young Americans tried to get back to more natural ways of living. Young mothers of all races commonly carried their infants on their backs, papoose style. Even today mothers transport babies in this manner. Baby stores in modern malls sell baby carriers. These are much like cradleboards without all the special decorations.

Another creature comfort for the newborn was a hammock, or sling, hung across the lodge. This Indian invention is still used today. Even in a modern city apartment, a young Indian mother often has a baby sling hung across her living room. These hammocks could also hold a mother or father who wanted to sway while cuddling baby. In the rain forest of South America, Indian hammocks are big enough for even a sister or brother to scooch in! Those of us who have had infants in our homes know how much they like to swing. Imagine if we could swing with them cuddled close.

Children among the Native Americans did not want for anything. Their world was surrounded by creature comforts and loving souls. They were not excluded from company at home and placed in a room alone at night. They were able to become familiar with the sounds of the family and visiting relatives and friends, and they learned to sleep in this way. Of course, children and adults were never loud at these times, having been trained to be always mindful of others.

But, if sleep still became a problem for the babies, special lullabies were sung, and their magic lulled the little restless ones to sleep. Even today, parents who don't know the songs will play a record or cassette tape of Indian music. It can often fulfill the purpose.

During important ceremonies, especially the presentation of the sacred pipe, all people were expected to be respectful and silent. If a baby cried, the pipe was often carried to the fussing child and waved over its head while a special soothing song was sung. After the baby quieted down, the ceremony continued.

CHAPTER 3

The Freest Life in the World

▲▲▲

Ho! Ye Winds, Clouds, Rain, Mist, all ye that move in the air, I bid you hear me!

Into your midst has come a new life. Consent ye, I implore!

Make its path smooth, that it may reach the brow of the second hill!

— from the Omaha Indian song, "Introduction of the Child to the Universe"

Almost all boys like to play Indian. For most children, being an Indian child means you are as free and as close to nature as a butterfly.

Parents today are quick to leave the city with their children for a vacation in a national park or a nearby campsite. In many ways, they are trying to keep in touch with nature, and they use Indian inventions to help them: the sleeping bag, the hammock, the canoe, and even snowshoes and toboggans and snow goggles. Yes, a kid today eating freshly caught fish and corn-on-the-cob cooked over an open fire with Dad and Mom can experience a small but vital part of being Native American. That part is simply being close to family and to nature.

Indian children were never scolded for going out in the pouring rain and playing in the soft, wet, muddy earth. They were aware of the Thunder Beings, of course. If these great giants that flash lightning from their eyes were nearby, the children went indoors for safety.

The outdoor life was where much of the action occurred. Indian boys played hunting games and war games, and they tested each other's bravery all the time. Even the girls would participate, for Indian children were rarely, if ever, told that girls could not play war games. In fact, among some of the People, there are stories of women warriors.

One woman warrior was a leader among the Shawnee. Her name was Tall Soldier Woman. During the Shawnee's many battles with the invading United States soldiers, Tall Soldier Woman was the leader of the warriors from her village.

In many of the tribes, boys were encouraged to handle dolls in order to help them develop into nurturing adults who would be gentle with babies of their own. Among the Hopi, all children, including boys, were encouraged to play with Katchina dolls. This not only fostered good parenting, but the children became familiar with the different Katchinas, which represented the various societies within the Hopi culture that the boys would one day be invited to join.

In short, children most often made their own choice of play. The Indian way was not to interfere with a child's development, but to teach and give guidance.

Yet, there were some things that boys and girls were told not to do. The People had their reasons. It was unthinkable for an Indian parent to say you can't do something because "I told you so." There were reasons. In most tribes, for instance, the warriors' drum was not to be touched by a girl or a woman. The reasoning was understandable. On this drum were sung war songs and, therefore, songs of death. The Indian female was a giver of life. The two powers could clash, hurting them both.

This, however, did not mean that the women could not have drums. On the contrary, Indian nations had societies that were strictly for women, and they even had drums that only they could beat. The late Princess Red Wing of the Narragansett Tribe, Wampanoag Nation, had a drum that only she used. Before she died, she passed this drum on to a young girl. She told the young girl that boys could hold it and sing with it, but only if the girl consented.

Other than rules about things such as that, Indian children were as free as anyone on earth to play as they wished. Problems did occur, however, when the children became so involved with their activities that the whole village wound up putting the pieces back together again. A Kiowa story that Alice Marriott tells in *The Ten Grandmothers* clearly shows how children and mischief sometimes go together.

The story really happened this way. It was during the time when the Kiowa country was being invaded by soldiers. The soldiers came with guns, and the warriors fought them hard.

At first, the fighting usually took place far from the village. The warriors would intercept the troops. They did this far away from their village, for the warriors knew what soldiers did to women and children of Indian villages if they had the chance. The warriors knew their women and children would be safe only if the soldiers stayed away.

Well, one day a Kiowa war party, led by the great chief White Bear, did battle with the soldiers and won a fiercely contested fight. The Kiowa chiefs and braves were a long time in returning home, but they sang victory songs along the way and joked with each other. They anticipated the welcome they would receive in the village. This was a rare battle in which no Kiowa warriors had been killed.

You see, fighting the soldiers was different from fighting Indians of other tribes. In the old days, Indians rarely killed each other in battle. No one liked killing. For the United States soldiers, killing was the only kind of fighting they were trained for. Anyway, in this particular battle, White Bear had captured an army bugle and was eager to show it off back at the village. He was especially eager to blow on it.

Their Kiowa village was in a safe place, surrounded by water on three sides. It was safe because an enemy attack could come from only one side. This made it very defendable from the enemy, but in the opinion of the children it was not quite safe enough. The Kiowa girls had played the enemy that day, and the boys were the Kiowa warriors. When that game was over, they decided to all go on a war party, but they just couldn't leave the women and small children without protection.

So, they had the grand idea of digging a ditch along the only accessible side of the village. In this way, they could keep out the enemy and protect the horses that were corralled on the village side of the ditch. It was a great plan, and the boys and girls all worked hard making it a very fine ditch, and deep too. They used the dirt they had dug up to build a wall on one side of the ditch from behind which the People could defend themselves. Too bad it got dark and everyone had to go home.

That night, White Bear couldn't wait to blow his newly acquired government-issue U.S. Cavalry bugle, so he did. Sound on the plains travels far, especially at night, and the women back in the village recognized it immediately.

Fear spread, and everyone prepared to escape an attack. The women and girls rolled up the teepees, and the boys put out the fires and helped the men get their weapons. Then they headed for the horses.

All of a sudden, there was this terrible commotion of screaming animals and excited men. Bodies were falling on bodies. The men and boys were scurrying for their lives in the grand pit, the ditch the boys had forgotten about. Horses fell around them and sometimes on them. Then the horses stampeded the village.

Sunrise the next day seemed to come ever so slowly. It was like the mighty sun didn't want to see what had happened that night. Fortunately, none of the People was seriously hurt. But the place was a mess, and when White Bear rode in with his shiny brass bugle, his pride at having captured it and winning the battle changed into utter bewilderment. The People just shook their heads at him and the war party, and grumbled about blowing bugles at night.

The village was finally put back together. The caller gathered all the People together, and they made a rule that only men could build ditches. Men would know where the ditches were. That was it. The kids were not punished or scolded or beaten. The children did manage to stay busy for some time afterwards, away from the shaking heads and piercing eyes of the adults.

Of course, Native American children had all kinds of games beside those that had to do with the protection of the tribe. One of the most popular children's games is "follow the leader." In this particular game, the bravest and strongest child would be the leader. He would take the others on an endurance and courage-testing adventure. Their knowledge of nature would grow during these games as they traveled through muddy swamps, up steep hills, across hot, sandy earth, and even through streams and lakes, where their ability to swim became part of the game. In such a game, boys and girls would play together. Or, if they chose, some games could be just for girls or for boys.

The idea of segregated games for only boys or girls is often criticized by modern people. They think that having sexual roles and taboos is backward. Although Indian adults guided children, they never forced them into sexual roles. The child decided which role to play. The People accepted the child's decision, and there were no slang words to ridicule that choice.

Indian children were taught that Sky is Father and Earth is Mother and that the Great Mystery is neither male nor female, but aspects of both. Sky and Earth — one cannot flourish without the other. Each has a separate role, but each is equal to the other. For an Indian girl to learn weaving or cooking was no less an art form or responsibility than for an Indian boy to learn arrow-making or hunting. In the tribe, as well as in nature, there was balance.

Nature was the grand teacher. In clearing a field for cultivation, for example, it was often the tradition for the men to do the clearing. A field is cleared by killing, by uprooting grasses and weeds, or even by removing trees. Killing plants was still killing, and men were the killers. Once the field was cleared, the women and girls began their work. Usually they planted the seeds in the gardens. They were the givers of life. These were different tasks, but equal roles.

Nature and the elders taught Indian boys one more lesson: their foremost responsibility was to protect, provide for, and defend the women and girls.

Of all the games, the children probably liked ball games the best. One game, played in one form or another by Native American people across the country, is known today as *lacrosse*, a physically brutal game of endurance, teamwork, and agility. Men of the tribe would defend their goal against another clan, or team, of the same tribe. The children often got into their own contests of lacrosse. Women and girls had their own version of the game, too.

An elderly Iroquois man, Ray Fadden of the Six Nations Museum in the state of New York, is one of the most knowledgeable Indian historians in the country. He once told the story of the first time the white man ever saw a rubber ball. He explains that the early Europeans thought it was alive. In their own words, the Spaniards described rubber as "a sap made into balls which bounced and looked as if they were alive." The rubber tree grew throughout Central and South America and was used for generations by Indians from there, and the North American Indians acquired rubber through trade.

It didn't take long for Indian-style ball games and even ice games to become important parts of national and international sports. Not many people today know that Indian children raced and played in their toboggans long before any other children in the world did so. The Native American children loved contests that tested mental and physical abilities.

Another beloved competition was racing. When the children weren't racing their horses, they had foot-races with each other. Some of the greatest long-distance runners in the world have been Native Americans. Millions of television viewers watched as long-distance runner Billy Mills won the Olympics. Even today, years after his death, Jim Thorpe is regarded as one of the greatest world-class runners and all-around athletes. American sportswriters selected him as the greatest athlete of the first half of the twentieth century.

The Indian child was raised differently than is a child today. The Indian child was taught to be competitive, but not in the way a child is in these times. The Indian child was always instructed to develop in ways that would be beneficial to the whole People, not simply to himself. The Indian child did not win glory for himself. He won glory for his people.

These Native American contests and games were designed to help a child learn control over him or herself, not dominance over others and nature. He was not taught to fight against the natural elements, but to work in harmony with them, to feel one with all things. He was not a separate being forcing himself on or against something else. The Indian children learned respect for their fellow brothers, sisters, cousins, and friends by learning that different people have different abilities. These differences made no one better or worse than anyone else.

Each Native child was taught to contribute to the welfare of the People. Each was taught that he or she had something to offer the People. There was simply no place in the nation for a person who refused to contribute to the good of the People.

CHAPTER 4

Earning an Indian Name

▲▲▲

Ho! Ye Hills, Valleys, Rivers, Lakes, Trees, Grasses, all ye of the earth, I bid you hear me!

Into your midst has come a new life. Consent ye, I implore!

Make its path smooth, that it may reach the brow of the third hill!

— from the Omaha Indian song, "Introduction of the Child to the Universe"

Indian names are special. They are symbols of power given in special ways. Indian names carry stories of how they came to be. They can be passed down. They can be earned. They can come from dreams and visions. Indian names reveal a special relationship to nature and the Great Mystery.

One of the most special events in a traditional Native American's life is the giving of a name. This tradition varied somewhat from tribe to tribe and from individual to individual.

Some nations, such as the Hopi, gave the baby the name that seemed most suited to it. This name came from one of the child's aunts. Among other nations, and no doubt among the Hopi too, there were certain people who were dreamers, and they could call on their dreams for names of children.

Other nations, such as the Lakota, attached little importance to a child's first name. It was merely a sound the child would answer to. Later on, the child would be given another name. This name could stick for the rest of the child's life, or it could change. The name revealed certain aspects of the child's nature and maybe even a story about the child's life.

It was also a practice among some of the People to pass on names from old to young. Crazy Horse is an example of this. Crazy Horse, as a small boy, was called "Curly." This name came from his brown, curly hair. It was a child's name. When Curly became a man, his father passed the name Crazy Horse to him. His father knew that his son deserved and needed a name of power. Crazy Horse's father then took the name "Worm." It was a humble yet proud name for an elder getting ready to return his body to Mother Earth.

A most powerful name was one that came in a dream or vision. Among nearly all Native Americans, a boy was trained from early in life to seek a vision. This was done by fasting from food and water and concentrating on one's relationship to the Great Mystery. The vision-seeking was a test of sorts, not only of courage, but of the sincerity of one's heart. Without a vision, an Ojibwa boy could never attain true manhood. He was considered "half a man." An adult Indian male without a vision to follow or pursue could not be trusted. The vision enabled him to be a positive force within the tribe. It also allowed him true Power, and using it would help his people.

Not all powerful Indian names resulted from vision-seeking, but all true Indian names were earned. An Indian didn't want to earn a name that would cause him embarrassment. He wanted his enemies to speak his name with fear, his friends and allies to speak it with respect.

Some Indians had as many as three names in their lifetimes. First, there was the one given at birth. Then there was another that was earned by the elders' observations of the child's behavior. Finally, there would be the name that the young Indian or one of the elders saw or heard in a vision or great dream.

Indian names linked the People to nature — to the animals, birds, trees, or even insects — or to the cosmic entities of Sun, Moon, and Stars. They established a special relationship with one special being. Each one was a name for just one person. If an Indian did not pass his or her name on, it left when he or she died.

One Ojibwa baby girl was named Nag-we-yabik (*nag-way-yaa beek*), or Rainbow. A poem was written for her to read when she grew older and had the need:

> Colored Lines
> Connecting Things and Places —
> circular symbol of beauty —
> Return of the Blessing
> and Fertility;
>
> Rainbow,
> your name is all this,
> to guide you
> and be your source
> of Power.
> And one day when it is
> dark and stormy (as life
> can be from time to time)
> there will be within
> your name, Nag-we-yabik,
> that special meaning for only
> you to find.

Today, children of all colors and ages often desire an Indian name. It's no wonder, because it's so special!

To raise Native American children in these times is difficult, for much of the true Indian philosophy and

history has been ignored or ridiculed by modern man. The Indian child sees his own race made into a silly cartoon caricature named "Chief Wahoo" by the Cleveland Indian's baseball team. It's hard for an Indian child to rise above that idea of his race and to be proud.

To be an Indian child today, one must learn to respect those elders who have the wisdom of life and of the past. The children must be taught to respect those elders enough to learn from them the ways of the People. All of these ways have to do with respect — respect for one's self, one's people, other people, and all things. Indian children were not taught to love all things, but to seek understanding, because understanding creates love.

Whether a Native American family lived in a chickee in Florida, a wigwam in Manitoba, a teepee on the Great Plains, or a hogan in the Southwest, none of these homes required locks to protect property from theft. Every Indian child was taught to respect the space and property of others, and he or she could rest comfortably knowing that this respect prevailed among the People of any nation. It was the universal law.

Today, the Native American child must also learn the power of the language that his ancestors understood. Whether it be a foreign tongue such as English, Spanish, or French, or a Native one, such as Cree, Seminole, or Arapaho, the children must use language with truth in their hearts. They must use it to express their thoughts and gratitude to the concept of the Great Mystery. The Great Mystery is their ancestors' abstract idea of the source and origin of the Universe. In the Mystery all things share equal importance, and all things are part of the Great Mystery. The children must gather around the drums when they can, dance their feelings of life when they can, and listen to the melodies of the flute.

All this will help join the Native children more closely with the power of *Orenda*. Orenda is a spirit power that summons the greatness of the ancestors. It enables the living to ward off evil and to make good happen. The power of Orenda will keep the Native Americans strong. Unless the Native child is raised in the ways of the People, the People will be no more!

Ho! Ye Birds, great and small, that fly in the air,

Ho! Ye Animals, great and small, that dwell in the forest,

Ho! Ye Insects that creep among the grasses and burrow in the ground, I bid you hear me!

Into your midst has come a new life. Consent ye, I implore!

Make its path smooth, that it may reach the brow of the fourth hill!

Ho! All ye of the heavens, all ye of the air, all ye of the earth, I bid you hear me!

Into your midst has come a new life. Consent ye, I implore!

Make its path smooth — then shall it travel beyond the four hills!

PART II

By the Magic of the Strawberry Moon

▼▼▼

CHAPTER 1

Because They Loved the Earth

From the north direction it has rained. From the west direction the water comes in streams . . . . All of us receive life. Now, chief, for this life-giving rain, you must love the earth . . . .

—from a song of the Keres Pueblo
to a new chief

▼▼▼

The Tomaquag Indian Museum was — empty! Only Caddo and Violet, his older sister, were there. He was admiring an old gourd rattle displayed in a glass case. She was sniffing a lovely sweetgrass basket hanging from a log beam. Suddenly, they heard a voice.

"Because they loved the Earth, we live today."

"Did you hear that?" Caddo whispered, adjusting his wire-rimmed glasses. Violet nodded. Their eyes flicked nervously about, searching the dimly lit room. "It sounded like a man."

"Too many movies," she mumbled. It was her first year as a teenager, Violet thought, and she didn't need this.

"Because they loved the earth, we live today!" Again a voice! It spoke the same words, only this time it sounded like a woman.

"Who's there? Who *is* that?" Violet called. She felt like she was speaking in some sort of vacuum. Her words didn't seem to have any vibration. There was no echo — only dead silence.

Suddenly, two shadows appeared in the dark of the room. Slowly, they moved into the dim light. The children's eyes were wide with terror until the shadowy figures became a harmless-looking old man and a gentle-looking old woman.

The old man wore thick glasses that magnified his eyes. His white and silver hair was pulled back into a thin ponytail.

The old woman was bent forward. She wore a tender smile on a wrinkled face. The silver bracelet on her frail wrist was the color of her hair.

The old man looked at the gourd rattle in the case near Caddo. "Because they loved the earth, we live today," he said again. Caddo just blinked his eyes. "Sorry, we didn't mean to startle you. We're so old, and with things the way they are today — well, we were a little afraid of you, too."

"Who are you?" Caddo demanded. "Where'd you come from?"

"Oh," the old woman said, "we used to come here when we were kids — just like you — and listen to the stories."

Violet folded her arms. "What stories?" she asked, rolling her eyes. "There's no one else here."

The old people glanced about the room. "Appears you're right," said the man, fixing a gaze on Violet with his magnified eyes. Something about them made her uncomfortable.

"Maybe we should go," she said. "I mean, it's nearly three, and school's almost out."

"Shhh!" whispered Caddo. But it was too late. Thanks to Violet, their skipping school was no longer a secret. Besides, it wasn't the first time they'd come to the Tomaquag Museum to spend a school day. They figured that sooner or later they'd get caught.

The old people glanced at each other and laughed quietly.

Caddo seized the moment. "You mean you're not gonna turn us in?"

"Truth is," explained the old man, "we used to do the same thing. Why, coming here was one of the best things in our lives."

"Yes," added the old woman, "we thought we'd come back one last time to hear the stories. But, like you said, there's no one else here but us."

"Yeah, but you must remember something!" said Caddo.

"Let it be!" Violet said sternly to her brother. Her teeth were clenched, and her eyes squinted suspiciously. "Let's just go and leave these folks to their memories."

"Wait. Don't go yet," insisted the old man. "My older sister and I want you to stay."

"Yes, please stay," pleaded the woman. "It's my brother's and my last visit. This would make it so special."

Caddo stared mercilessly at Violet until she nodded her approval, though somewhat reluctantly. "OK," she muttered, "just for a while."

Little did they know how special the day was to become, for in every gourd and every basket and every piece of pottery in that old museum was something that Indians call *Orenda*, a spiritual power from the past that happens now!

CHAPTER 2

Food of the Sachems

My children, when at first I liked the whites,
My children, when at first I liked the whites,
I gave them fruits,
I gave them fruits.

> — from a southern Arapaho
> ghost dance song

▼▼▼

"Imagine if all these things could speak," said Caddo. Violet laughed at such a foolish idea. But then, she figured, ever since her brother made it to sixth grade, he had weird ideas about ghosts and spirits and such. Like the time they were alone and Caddo thought he saw a ghost outside the house. It turned out to be only his reflection in the window. At least, that's what Violet said,

never admitting that she also had that feeling of another presence.

"Oh!" exclaimed the old woman. "But they can."

"Can what?" demanded Violet.

"These things here . . . the baskets and bowls and gourds — they *do* speak. Take that basket there," she said, pointing to a case labeled CENTRAL AMERICAN INDIAN ART. "It probably carried all kinds of vegetables and fruits."

Violet's voice got higher. "You mean Indians back then had those things?"

"Oh my, yes!" laughed the old man. "And much more. Why, our ancestors developed most of the foods that feed the world today. As a matter of fact, over half the world's food staples are American Indian. And, if that doesn't impress you, almost all the food we eat in this country today was cultivated by our American Indian ancestors."

Caddo and Violet spent the next few seconds digesting what they had just heard. Then, Caddo realized something the old man had said. He called Indians "our" ancestors. That meant he must be an Indian. "So you're Indians too," Caddo declared. The old people smiled and nodded. Caddo smiled proudly. "I was even named for a tribe," he added.

"Me too," said the man sadly, "a tribe that exists no more, except in the memory of my name."

Violet figured she understood why the old people said they could hear the gourds and the baskets and such. "You can hear these things speak because you're Indians." She glanced again at the case of Central American Indian art. "What do they say?"

"They say," the old man began, "Imagine what Italian food would taste like without tomatoes. What would we put on spaghetti to make it so good if there were no tomato sauce? What would pizza be like? Imagine even more what a hamburger would taste like without ketchup. Sure, at Burger King you can say, 'Hold the onions, extra pickles, and just a little lettuce,' but who has ever heard someone say, 'No ketchup'?"

"And what would life be like without tomato soup and sandwiches," added the old woman, "not to mention a salad bar with no tomatoes?"

Violet laughed. "Is that what they're really saying?"

"Yes," he said. Then he narrowed his eyes and looked at Caddo. "There are even some kids, like me when I was one, who like to sprinkle a little salt on a tomato and eat it just that way!"

"I do that!" exclaimed the boy.

"What a treat!" smiled the old man. "It's no wonder the People called the tomato 'the food of the sachems (chiefs).' " He glanced at Violet, then back to Caddo. "It's that special, you know." And they nodded.

"Strange," he continued, "how tomato plants grew in the Old World as well as here in our country. They come from a family of plants called the nightshade. These can be poisonous, you know. That's why the first Europeans must have been suspicious when the Native people offered them tomatoes in these baskets as gifts of food. They didn't know that the American Indians, through their love for the earth, through their knowledge of agriculture, and through their dreams, could have cultivated such a deadly plant and made its fruits good to eat.

" — Which reminds me of a horror story of the worst kind. It was told to me by an old man a long time ago." He leaned forward, resting on the glass case of gourd rattles but looking at the baskets all the while, as if they, or that something called Orenda, was speaking to him out of the past. "You kids like scary stories?"

They nodded and began to fidget with nervous anticipation.

"Well," he began, "when I was . . ." he paused and gazed at Caddo curiously, "in the sixth grade — just like you — I skipped school and came here as usual with my sister. We found this old man in here — like me."

"Wait!" cried the woman. "I remember. There was a very old lady with him. I thought she was the oldest person I'd ever seen!" She blinked, startled at something she suddenly felt.

"Yes, it's true," the man agreed, shaking his head as if to clear it. "They were both very old."

"Anyway, somehow this strange old man asked us, like I did you, if we liked scary stories, and we said yes, just like you. Only the story he was to tell, he said was true. I can't remember what day it is, but I can recall that moment as if it happened yesterday.

"The People tell of a time," he began, "when the first white man set foot on our land. They were called Spaniards, and they carried with them a cross. They recorded their voyages, their conquests, and what they saw in their journals for generations to read. Our people recorded encounters with these strange new people in our memories. Those times will never be forgotten.

"They describe when the Spanish first arrived in this land and how they were greeted by friendly, healthy, and happy natives. Even Columbus wrote back to the king and queen of Spain that a more beautiful and peaceful nation did not exist in the world. 'They love their neighbors as themselves,' Columbus said. But the Spaniards were cruel in their treatment of these 'peaceful' people. Their cruelty brought shame to mankind, something like what Hitler did to the Jews.

"Nevertheless, the old one said, the Native Americans saw these new people as brothers. They greeted them on the shores of our homeland with baskets filled with food. Among the great variety of vegetables and fruits that the Spaniards had never seen was something indeed familiar — tomatoes. But to them, tomatoes were poisonous.

"So, the old man asked me, 'What do you think those Spaniards did?' I just shook my head. 'They cut off the Indians' hands!' he said. They thought the Indians were trying to poison them. Our people didn't understand."

Violet's jaw dropped in horror. Feeling suddenly queasy, she sat on the log bench near the case. The old woman gently touched Violet's shoulder, and she rested her face against the woman's hand. It felt old and soft and precious. Caddo's lips tightened and his fists clenched. His warrior spirit struggled to hold back his anger, while the old man's large watery eyes stared blankly at the empty baskets.

CHAPTER 3

The Day of the Very Great Feast

Long ago you never found half a village hungry, jobless, and homeless while the other half lived in luxury. The chief saw to it that everybody worked, cooperated, and made the village liveable and prosperous. If crops were poor, all suffered alike and long were their prayers and appeals to the Great Spirit.

— from Princess Red Wing's
History of the Indian's Religion

"Peanuts, popcorn, and potato chips. Vanilla and chocolate. Chewing gum. Maple sugar, maple syrup. Ice cream cones! Sure. Ice cream cones were first enjoyed by our Indian ancestors. Parents used to make a cone and gather fresh snow to put in it. Then they'd dip the cone in maple syrup and give it to their children to enjoy. The Pilgrim parents tried it, and their kids loved it too.

"And can you imagine the first time a white man tasted a pumpkin pie? That must have been a sight! Even pineapple comes from the Indians. It wasn't always grown in Hawaii, you know. It was cultivated first by the Indians of Mexico and then brought over to Hawaii."

The children's mouths watered and their minds filled with wonder as the old man ran off the list of some of their favorite snacks. It was like he kept it somewhere in his head and could call it up at will.

"All gifts," he said. "All were gifts of the Indians. Think what our world today would be like without the food they developed."

"Just awful," Violet grumbled. "It would sorta take the fun out of living, I mean, when you think about it."

"Yeah," agreed Caddo. "I can't imagine not having any of that stuff in the world!"

"We had it all!" exclaimed the old man. "We were healthy and happy. We didn't even have many diseases until the white man came. Yet, when you see one of those pictures, like that one on the wall above the gourd case there, the Indian is always pictured as having to look up at the Pilgrims. In fact, it was the other way around!

"Why, that old man I met told me there are records of all this. Some even say that the average height of the European when he first landed in this country was just over five feet. A junior high student today would have trouble fitting into a suit of Spanish armor. And, if you've ever seen one of those pilgrim houses that's preserved for history, either of you might have to duck to get through the doorway. He told me, like I'm telling you now, that one out of every ten of those early colonists was born with some deformity — mental or physical — because of their poor diet and living conditions.

"They were in no way as healthy back then as they are now. I ask you, what would the white man have become without the Indian?

"Think on it. When the Wampanoags greeted the Pilgrims on these shores, the Indians were the ones strong and healthy. Then smallpox came with the slave traders and wiped the Indians out; that is, all those who weren't killed by guns or slavery. Some fled west and joined other tribes; others simply ran away and hid, their fields and crops taken over by the Pilgrims."

It seemed unthinkable for the children to interrupt this old man who kept in his memory the things he was taught as a child, especially those feelings that somehow are remembered in the blood and have a way of making history come alive. No, neither Violet nor Caddo would speak, even if they had something to add, at least not while the old man was still talking. He would just walk around that ancient museum and talk about the things he saw.

In a very real way, the old woman was right when she said these wonderful baskets and gourds and pots and cooking utensils can talk. They must have talked to him, for when he was speaking, his words kept flowing like a river of knowledge.

The old woman sat with Violet on the log bench. "Thanksgiving," she said. "Now, there's a time when Native Americans are remembered. Though it was some sixty years ago, it seems like yesterday when our class dressed up as either Indians or Pilgrims and played games most of the day.

"At lunch, we moved all our desks, made one giant table, and ate together, sharing all the goodies we brought from our homes. Our moms stayed up late the night before, preparing each food. We called it 'the day of the very great feast.' "

Violet seemed shocked. "That's really weird," she said. "About three years ago, when I was in fourth or fifth grade — I can't remember exactly — we did the same things. We even called it 'the day of the very great feast.' Or, maybe it was something like that."

"That *is* weird," added Caddo.

"Maybe it's just a coincidence," the old woman said.

"Yeah," agreed Violet. "I suppose 'the day of the very great feast' is a pretty common name for kids to think up."

The old woman smiled, but she seemed puzzled. Was there more to it than coincidence, she wondered? In any case, she collected herself and resumed the Thanksgiving story. "Well," she said, "I remember one little girl who brought cranberries, and another brought sweet potatoes. Bobby Harris brought the squash and ate most of it too." She laughed.

Violet wasn't laughing, but she turned and stared at the old woman with wide, frightened eyes. She had also known a boy in fourth grade named Bobby Harris. At least, she thought his name was Bobby Harris. Maybe it was Bobby Harrison. She figured that had to be the case, as her memory for details was not as sharp as the old woman's. But Bobby Harris sure sounded right.

"We brought pumpkin bread," the old woman continued, "pumpkin pies, and green beans. It was just a truly great feast for everyone, and all with American Indian food! Even the turkey our teacher brought was Native American."

Then, as if she suddenly saw something awful, she frowned. Her eyes were sad and her voice was sorrowful, even bitter. "I didn't know," she said. "I just didn't know that the People had their stories too. They tell how the Pilgrims wouldn't allow the Indians to sit with them at that first Thanksgiving," she said. "I didn't know until that day when the old woman told me, like I'm telling you. She described how they 'let' our people serve them the very food we brought for the feast."

She continued to speak of the hard winter Governor Bradford and his Pilgrim people had. She explained that many Pilgrims died that harsh winter and that the crops the Indians had helped them plant also died. "When

Squanto overheard Governor Bradford crying to God about his hard loss," she said, "Squanto told the governor to cease his crying. He said that now, more than ever, he should send thanks to his God for those who did survive. He told him that with what little food they had managed to harvest, they should hold a celebration. 'Now's the time to rejoice the most!' Squanto said.

"Well," she continued, "the Pilgrims didn't know that the Indians had a Thanksgiving every one of the thirteen full moons that make up a yearly cycle. No, we didn't give thanks to Mother Earth just once a year, but once a month. Lucky for those Pilgrims that one of the four most important was near to happening. It was the Harvest Thanksgiving.

"So, following Squanto's instructions, the Pilgrims gathered what little they had, and they prepared. You can imagine their expressions when our ancestors showed up with all that food! Most of it the Pilgrims had never even seen before!"

She paused briefly and pointed to a large black kettle displayed with other cooking utensils. "See that big kettle over there!" The children nodded. "Well, all kinds of food are in that kettle."

"Indeed!" said the old man. "Every variety of bean in the world, except soybean, are in that pot, gifts of American Indians. Those world-famous Boston baked beans are really Wampanoag or Iroquois baked beans with a company label."

"Yes," the old woman said, "in that kettle can be cooked many gifts of food, not only from Native Americans, but from all over the world. For people to forget this is wrong. Just imagine a great stew simmering with the inviting scent of delicious food!

"Imagine the day of the Pilgrims' first Thanksgiving. It must have been the day of a very great feast, indeed!"

CHAPTER 4

The Strawberry Moon

The moon is setting,
At either side are bamboos for arrow-
making,
  Beside the bamboos are wildcat babies,
  They walk uncertainly,
  That is all.

  — A charm against sickness,
    from the Papago Indians

▼▼▼

The old man smiled. His eyes stretched the entire width of his glasses. "So you say you kids like stories? Well, this birch-bark basket has one. You know, it used to carry lots of strawberries!"

Violet sighed and tried to appear brave. "Is it another horror story?" she asked, swallowing her fear. The story of the Spaniards hacking off the hands of the Indians who brought them tomatoes was still in her mind. It's the kind of story that mingles with the blood and becomes memory. It would always be there.

"So what?" exclaimed Caddo. "We need to know the Indian side of things." He stood straight and looked at the old man. "Tell us your story. I'm not afraid."

Violet wriggled on the bench and sat up straight, flicking her hair back defiantly. "Me either. Besides, I never said I was scared." The old woman patted the girl's knee. Violet's lips pursed together. "Brothers!" she puffed.

"Well then, I'll tell you the story of the Strawberry Moon."

"What's a strawberry moon?"

"Hmmm," said the old woman, thinking hard on Violet's question. "Remember when my brother explained how Indians gave thanks to Mother Earth and the Great Mystery every full moon?" Both children nodded. "Well, if you look on the bottom of any turtle, you should be able to count thirteen squares. Those squares represent each of the thirteen full moons. Each tribal people had a name for those moons, or months, much like we do today. Only instead of the thirteen moons that make up a year, we now have twelve months and a leap year! Anyway, instead of calling them the Melting Snow Moon or the Acorn Moon, we have names today like March and September."

"How do you know all this stuff?" asked Caddo.

"The old people told us like we're telling you now," explained the old man. "And I'll never forget the story of the Strawberry Moon."

"Why?" asked Violet.

The old woman touched her cheek. "Because," she said, "if you're like my brother and me, you can get into some nasty quarrels — and sometimes over the littlest things."

"You mean like what just happened to me and my brother about me being scared."

"Oh my, yes. That's why this story is one you'll like."

"A long, long time ago," the old man began, "when people were still new in the world, two children lived with their grandmother. They were brother and sister.

"Much of the time they would get along with each other. But when they quarreled, it was just awful. It got so bad that sometimes the grandmother would just cry. One day, they were arguing about something and saw that their behavior was making their grandmother sad and sick. So, they decided to leave and never see one another again.

"She headed west with the sun at her back. He headed east with the sun before him. They grumbled and muttered for some time about how they just couldn't live together anymore.

"Well, as the sun shined on the girl's face and warmed the back of the boy, they lost track of what they had argued about. Crows cawed at them. And as the sun set and the star-quilt of night drew across the sky, the boy became afraid for the safety of his sister. She, likewise, felt responsible for her younger brother's welfare. She became frightened that something would happen to him.

" 'I could never forgive myself,' she cried, sitting among the straw and grasses that grew about.

"Her brother was too worried to go on without his sister. So, he decided to try and find her.

"The moon was full and high when the girl fell to the ground, her heart beating upon the earth. 'Grandmother Moon,' she wept, 'I'm so sorry. If only I had something to show my brother how sorry I truly am.'

"The Moon told her to look down. When she did, her eyes went wide! There, among the straw and grasses, were bright red berries. Quickly she gathered them and headed back in hopes of finding her brother.

"It was morning before she arrived at the lodge. Only her grandmother was there, sprinkling water on her face to wash away her tears and worry. When the old woman saw the bright red berries and heard what her granddaughter intended to do with them, she gave her a beautiful birch-bark basket, like that one right there," the old man said, pointing to the museum case labeled NORTHEAST AMERICAN INDIAN ART.

"When her brother finally returned, he was greatly relieved. His sister was all right. He pledged to protect her always. She, on the other hand, held up her basket of strawberries and gave them as a peace offering.

"That's why, children, till this day we are always at peace when we eat our strawberries — for during the Strawberry Moon, we are all reminded that peace begins within the individual heart."

CHAPTER 5

Mother Corn and Sweet Potato

The largest case in the museum was set into the wall. It contained all kinds of cooking utensils, grinding tools, pots, baskets, and masks. It had the simple label MOTHER CORN.

"Don't look so surprised!" the old man said. "In hundreds of centuries, we Indians figured out every way to plant, grow, harvest, cook, and eat Mother Corn. She is the mother of all our food plants. She has sustained us all over this hemisphere for thousands of years in hard years, as well as good ones.

"Most people admit that Indians gave the world corn," he explained. "What they don't say is how your ancestors developed all of the hundreds of varieties of corn.

"During the eighteenth century," he continued, "the population of Italy nearly doubled as a direct result of their growing and eating Mother Corn.

"Mother Corn and potatoes have become the world's most important foods. And, just like corn, your ancestors developed every major kind of potato in the world."

The old man spoke the truth to the children, for even in China, sweet potatoes are now one of the most important foods, especially among the rural peasants. The people of Russia depend on potatoes. What would the countries of northern Europe eat, if it weren't for potatoes? Remember German potato salad? Even the Scandinavians rely on the Native American potato.

"Then why are French-fried potatoes called French?" asked Caddo.

"I don't really know," answered the old man honestly.

Violet had a thought. "Maybe they were the first white people to eat Indian fried potatoes."

"Or," suggested the old woman, "perhaps after it became popular among the French, other countries began eating potatoes fried that way. They called them French fries. They thought the fries came from France."

"It's like the Irish potato," said the old man. "The Irish were among the first white people to accept the potato as a dependable food source. They probably had little choice. Their country, like most European countries after the New World discovery, had suffered many severe famines. When their crops failed miserably, many people died.

"Then the Irish began raising potatoes in Ireland. Their health improved. The potato is high in vitamin C content. It also can withstand great varieties of climate and climate changing. It made the Irish a much healthier and happier people. It was also responsible for the tremendous growth in their population."

Again, the old man's words rang true, for in the mid-eighteenth century, when Ireland began cultivating American Indian potatoes, their population exploded. They went from three million people to eight million a hundred years later!

"As a matter of fact," he said, "American Indian potatoes, corn, and the rest of the Indian foods became the source of a world population explosion!

"It wasn't long before Ireland was stricken by great potato famines. They didn't plant the variety of potatoes that Indians, such as the Incas, had planted. Instead, they selected only some types of potatoes. These particular ones couldn't survive the drought that Ireland has from time to time. Had they planted a variety, they would have been assured that some kind of potato would have survived. Ireland would not have had famine and death."

The children marveled how the old man's words flowed. They were awed by all he knew.

"You know," he said, "when the Indians farmed, they didn't deplete the soil. They farmed in a way that enabled trees to return to fields that had been cleared for planting. It takes thousands of years for an inch of topsoil to form. One inch! In less than a hundred years of the white man's farming the Mississippi Valley, an estimated thirteen inches have washed away.

"When an Indian nation, such as the Incas, finished farming a certain plateau, the soil was richer than before they had planted it.

"What did those Native ancestors understand?" he asked softly, almost like he was speaking to himself.

"For one thing," Caddo said, "they knew enough to call corn 'Mother.'"

CHAPTER 6

The Mystery

May it be beautiful before me,
May it be beautiful behind me ...
May it be beautiful all around me.
In beauty it is finished.

> — "Beauty Way" chant,
> from the Navaho

How long the old man and woman and Caddo and Violet spent in the Tomaquag Indian Museum that day, no one knows, not even them. They only knew that the power of Orenda was all around.

Each had gone there because it was a special place. It was a magical world that linked the past to the present, the present to the future. The old couple had returned for one final visit to thank the ghosts of the old ones for

teaching them the stories. They were only kids, the ages of Violet and Caddo, when the old ones taught them. Age had sapped the strength of their bodies, but the stories were still as clear and strong as ever.

For years they traveled the country once belonging to their people. It still does belong to them, but not in the way it once did.

It is no longer the country where the People thrived. Many of the People no longer live healthy and productive lives. Instead, the People seem confused, unhealthy, and endangered. The old couple had always tried to dream of a way to help the People survive. But the dream never came, until now.

They didn't know they would meet their own ghosts in the dimly lit room of stored baskets, bowls, and utensils. Not until Caddo asked the old man what tribe he was named for, the one which no longer existed, and the old man said, "Caddo," did they know.

The old woman removed her silver bracelet and slid it onto Violet's wrist. "This is meant for you," she whispered. Violet stared at the precious silver ornament. On it were inlaid three flowers — violets.

Once the baskets and bowls had held Mother Corn and other foods. The old couple, like the ancestors, held the stories. All were necessary to nourish the young.

The old man smiled at his sister. She reached over and put her hand on his. Their circle was now complete.

They knew what the ancestors knew: Time, like all things, is of the Mystery.

ACKNOWLEDGMENTS

The "Native People, Native Ways" series would not have been accomplished without the support and assistance of my wife, Simone, and the sacrifices made by my loving children: Ihasha, Calusa, and Carises. Without Jay Johnson's belief in my work and Paige Graham's ability to work with draft after draft of each manuscript, and without Paige's constant reminders for me to listen to the ghost voices, these books would not reflect the quality that they have. I'm also grateful to the publishers of Beyond Words, Cynthia Black and Richard Cohn, who recognized the quality of the series and the needs that the books can help fulfill. Their proofreader, Marvin Moore, and Native American curriculum specialist, Chris Landon, fine-tuned the books in such a way as to make us all proud. And to Fred Brady and the other elders who sent their prayers into the Mystery that these books would become a reality for our children and grandchildren, I give my deepest gratitude. I would also like to thank my friend and agent, Sandra Martin, who continues to encourage me to write. I'm grateful to Shonto Begay for his spark of creativity that will help children to see Native people in a Native way. And lastly, I wish to acknowledge all the elders who took the time to teach me, and all the writers whose spirit enabled them to share what they too have learned from the Native People and Native Ways of this land.

ABOUT THE AUTHOR

Noted author and lecturer Gabriel Horn was given the name "White Deer of Autumn" by his uncles, Meta-comet and Nippawanock, and by Princess Red Wing of the Narragansett tribe, Wampanoag nation. He has taught in reservation schools, American Indian Movement (AIM) survival schools, public schools, and junior colleges. He helped develop the curriculum and was head teacher at the Red School House in St. Paul, Minnesota. He was cultural arts director of the Minneapolis American Indian Center from 1980 to 1982 and helped establish the Minneapolis American Indian Art Gallery and the Living Traditions Museum. For his work in Indian rights, he was nominated for the Human Rights Award in the state of Minnesota.

Gabriel Horn has a master's degree in English and currently devotes his time to lecturing, teaching, and writing. He is a teacher in Florida as well as a member of the National Committee on American Indian History and an advisor to the Native American national newspaper, *Indigenous Thought*. He lives on the Florida coast with his wife, Simone, an Ojibway, close to Mother Earth and the natural world that is so precious to him.

ABOUT THE ILLUSTRATOR

Shonto Begay is a Native American artist who specializes in multicultural illustrations. His other works include *The Mud Pony,* a Native American story, and *Lluvia,* a Hispanic children's book. He lives in Kayenta, Arizona, with his family. His illustrations for *Native People, Native Ways* accurately detail the traditional dress, architecture, and art of the many different Native tribes in the various regions of the Americas throughout history.

Other Native American Children's Books
from Beyond Words Publishing, Inc.

THE NATIVE AMERICAN BOOK OF KNOWLEDGE

Author: White Deer of Autumn
Illustrator: Shonto Begay
96 pages, $5.95 softcover, ages 10-12

Investigates the fascinating and controversial origins of the People, based on tales from various tribes, scientific evidence, and archaeological finds. Discusses several key figures in the Americas, including Deganawida, Hyonwatha, and others who have had a mystical and spiritual impact on the Native people.

THE NATIVE AMERICAN BOOK OF CHANGE

Author: White Deer of Autumn
Illustrator: Shonto Begay
96 pages, $5.95 softcover, ages 10-12

Common stereotypes of Native Americans are explored and debunked, while passing on our personal "shields" — positive points of view that tell ourselves and others who and what we are — is encouraged. An important look back in time that focuses on the People's interaction with whites: the conquests of the Toltec, Aztec, Mayan, and North American tribes are covered.

THE NATIVE AMERICAN BOOK OF WISDOM

Author: White Deer of Autumn
Illustrator: Shonto Begay
96 pages, $5.95 softcover, ages 10-12

Explores the fascinating belief system of the People, from the concept of the Great Mystery, or Wakan-Tanka, to the belief that all life is sacred and interrelated. A tribal medicine man visits a contemporary classroom and the children are amazed at what he has to tell them about the traditions and power of his people.

CEREMONY IN THE CIRCLE OF LIFE

Author: White Deer of Autumn
Illustrator: Daniel San Souci
32 pages, $8.95 softcover, ages 6-10

The story of nine-year-old Little Turtle, a young Native American boy growing up in the city without knowledge of his ancestors' beliefs. He is visited by Star Spirit, who introduces him to his heritage and his relationship to all things in the Circle of Life. Little Turtle also learns about nature and how he can help to heal the Earth.

THE GREAT CHANGE

Author: White Deer of Autumn
Illustrator: Carol Grigg
32 pages, $14.95 hardcover, ages 3-10

A Native American tale in which a wise grandmother explains the meaning of death, or the Great Change, to her questioning granddaughter. This is a story of passing on tradition, culture, and wisdom to the next generation. It is a moving tale for everyone who wonders about what lies beyond this life. Watercolor illustrations by internationally acclaimed painter Carol Grigg.

COYOTE STORIES FOR CHILDREN: TALES FROM NATIVE AMERICA

Author: Susan Strauss
Illustrator: Gary Lund
50 pages, $11.95 hardcover, $7.95 softcover, ages 6-12

Storyteller Susan Strauss has interspersed Native American coyote tales with true-life anecdotes about coyotes and Native wisdom. These stories illustrate the creative and foolish nature of this popular trickster and show the wisdom in Native American humor. Whimsical illustrations throughout.

SUGGESTED READINGS

Waldman, Carl. *Atlas of the North American Indian.* New York: Facts on File, 1985.

Waldman, Carl, and Molly Braun. *Encyclopedia of Native American Tribes.* New York: Facts on File, 1988.

Waldman, Carl. *Who Was Who in Native American History.* New York: Facts on File, 1990.